501 DIY
Supersavers

501 DIY Supersavers

Hints and tips to save you time
and money around the home

Pamela Donald

GUILD PUBLISHING
LONDON · NEW YORK · SYDNEY · TORONTO

Acknowledgements

It would be impossible to list everyone whose trade secrets or bright ideas ended up in this book. However, Merry Parsons of WH Smith (*Do It All*) and Kim Cave of Stanley Tools deserve a special mention for unstinting help where a specialist opinion on techniques or materials was needed. Thank you both.

This edition published
1991 by Guild Publishing
by arrangement with
Judy Piatkus (Publishers) Ltd

CN 1131

Printed in Great Britain

Contents

Introduction

This book was originally intended to complement those heavy duty DIY manuals which are rarely opened, but are invaluable nonetheless for propping up sofas with broken legs, serving as kneeling pads for low-level DIY jobs, weighting and clamping various items while the glue dries, anchoring shuddering pipes and providing effective draught stoppers where the wind is howling through.

It may on the other hand be the only volume which the reluctant but discerning handyperson will ever purchase, and with many sections – Decorative Paint Finishes for example – it should be all that is needed to complete the job from start to finish.

I love tips, and next to the pleasure of finding new ones is the delight in passing them on to like-minded homedwellers who object to unnecessary waste of their time and money.

Pamela Donald

Safety First

Hand Care

○ *Advance protection . . .*

1 Protect your hands and nails before tackling any grubby work. Smear in petroleum jelly (Vaseline) as a barrier cream right up to your forearms. Rub your nails along a moist bar of soap. The dirt will wash off easily afterwards.

○ *Cleaning and aftercare . . .*

2 Remove stubborn stains from hands by rubbing them over with a raw potato. Then add a teaspoon of sugar to the soapy water when washing, and all traces of grime will rinse off.

Here's a heavy-duty dirt shifter favoured by car mechanics: rub undiluted washing up liquid into your hands and let it dry on your skin for a couple of minutes before washing off in the usual way.

 To soften hands roughened by DIY work, make up a half-and-half mix of vegetable oil and sugar and allow it to soak in for five minutes. Rinse off with warm water.

 If your hands have become chapped and red, mix two parts Vaseline to one part boracic powder and rub in gently to relieve the soreness.

Avoiding Injury

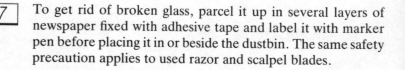

Use bread or damp cotton wool to pick up tiny fragments of broken glass safely.

To get rid of broken glass, parcel it up in several layers of newspaper fixed with adhesive tape and label it with marker pen before placing it in or beside the dustbin. The same safety precaution applies to used razor and scalpel blades.

When hammering in nails or tacks, protect your fingers from cuts and bruises by pushing the point through a piece of stiff cardboard. Use this as an extension of your fingers to hold the nail in place.

Always wear goggles when doing any work where dust or particles of debris may fly about and injure your eyes. A pinch of bicarbonate of soda in tepid water is the answer for washing out eyes. Methylated spirit will sparkle up the goggles.

10   It is always advisable to ventilate a room when painting, and when using solvents or solvent-based adhesives – when laying floor tiles, for example. However, fumes can penetrate clothes too, and standing close to an open fire in working overalls can turn a DIY duffer into a human torch. Water-based adhesives are safer, but take longer to dry.

See also 38, 67, 429.

First Aid

11   The best remedy for bruising is neat vinegar applied on a cotton wool pad. Secure with a bandage to the affected part until the dressing dries out.

12   If you're busy working out of doors, it's easy to become too absorbed to notice how a strong sun is catching you. A good sunburn cooler is bicarbonate of soda (baking soda), made into a paste, applied to the burn and covered with a light dressing to exclude air.

13   If you feel dizzy when working at a height or straining your neck muscles, press your thumbnail into the spot midway between your nostrils and upper lip.

14   In an emergency, egg white is good for slight burns. Run the affected part under cold water as soon as possible. Dry and cover in Vaseline. Extensive burns need proper medical treatment.

Sprains in knees and ankles should be treated immediately with an ice-cold compress to reduce the swelling. A cotton sock filled with ice cubes does admirably.

 To soothe aching joints and restore energy, relax in a hot bath with a handful of Epsom salts dissolved in the water.

 Treat stings with fluoride toothpaste to stop swelling and cure the itch.

18 There are two old wives' remedies for bee and wasp stings. Don't get them the wrong way round or you will aggravate the problem!
- ☐ B for bicarbonate treats bee stings.
- ☐ W for winegar (or vinegar) treats wasp stings.

19 When sewing or stitching, deal promptly with the problem of bloodstains from a pricked finger by chewing a length of white cotton thread and then rubbing the saliva-soaked cotton on to the blood. It will disappear without a trace.

Tools, Equipment and Useful Little Gadgets

20 Keep a house logbook with measurements of rooms, number of rolls of wallpaper needed, how many gallons of paint you used, plus snippets of curtain fabrics, wallpaper samples, shade cards and so on for quick and easy future reference. Also jot down the time it took to do the job – usually more than you thought.

21 It's worth paying extra for power tools which you know you will use on a regular basis. Then you can romp through the work in half the time. But never leave them plugged in when not in use – cordless varieties are safer and quicker to use.

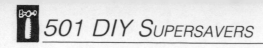

Hiring Equipment

 22 Some items which you may only use occasionally, such as floor sanders, wallpaper steamers or carpet stretchers, are better hired. Look up Hire Services in Yellow Pages or other local trade directories, and phone around to compare prices.

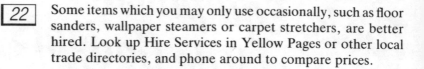 **23** For your own protection, only hire from a member of the Hire Association of Europe (HAE). Their many hire companies will give you advice on the best tools and equipment for the job. To get the best value when hiring, have everything ready for the job so that you can begin as soon as you collect the equipment.

Storing Stuff and Getting the Best Out of It

 24 If storing tools indefinitely, rub the metal bits with Vaseline and roll them in brown paper to keep them rust-free.

 25 Sharpen scissor blades by trying to cut the neck off a milk bottle, or else cut sandpaper with them.

 26 When hanging tools up on a wall, trace round the shape with a marker pen. You can then see at a glance what's missing.

 27 Wine bottle corks can be popped on the ends of sharp knives or other dangerously pointed tools as a protective shield.

28 A tape measure of the non-metal variety which has become the worse for wear can be stiffened up by ironing it between two pieces of waxed paper.

29 Aerosol cans, though handy to use, have an irritating habit of clogging up when only half empty. Remove the nozzle and place it in boiling water for a couple of minutes if the contents are soluble. Leave paint spray can nozzles in paraffin or paint stripper overnight.

30 When using rubber gloves for dirty work, you'll get maximum mileage from them if you wear them inside out or put sticking plaster across the tip inside the fingers to protect them from long nails.

31 Sponges won't crack or go slimy if they're washed in cold salted water, well wrung out, and then popped into polythene bags in between jobs.

32 Always work with sharp-bladed knives. They are actually safer than blunt ones, providing they are directed away from the body as you cut with them.

33 Always secure sheet material well so that it cannot slip and cause injury by 'riding up' when you are cutting it.

34 If you have trouble opening screw-top jars or bottles which have become encrusted but whose contents are still usable, try gripping the lid with sandpaper.

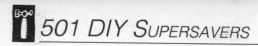

35   A wheelbarrow is useless for moving heavy things – it's too high off the ground and unstable when loaded. Buy instead a low-loading trolley. The secret when lifting bulky loads is to lever the weight. Use a plank of wood to help tip a bag on to a trolley. *See also 175.*

36   Get the last squeeze from a tube of adhesive, bath sealant or whatever by heating it through in hot water before you remove the cap.

Hammering, Nailing and Screwing

37   A small square of spare wood under a hammer head prevents damage and helps increase the leverage. Always hold the handle towards the end.

38 A dirty or shiny face on a hammer is likely to slip, causing damage to the object you're working on and/or injury to your person. Clean and condition it by placing a piece of sandpaper on a flat surface, pressing the hammer head on top and rubbing it in a circular movement on to the abrasive paper.

39 The longer the handle on hammers, wrenches and spanners, the greater the leverage and the less effort needed.

40 Nails versus screws. Nails are cheaper and quicker to use. Screws are stronger, allow dismantling more easily (for example, on boxed-in pipework which will need servicing) and give a neater appearance.

41 Here's a tip to prevent wood resisting and splitting, and to stop screws rusting and make them easier to remove should you ever have to. Dip the tips of screws and nails in pure beeswax polish or Vaseline, or press them into a bar of soap.

42 Loosen rusted screws or nails by first putting a drop of vinegar on the heads and leaving it to soak in. If this alone doesn't do the trick, the next step is to touch the head with a red-hot poker, or, in the case of screws, to insert a screwdriver into the head and tap firmly with a hammer.

43 The rule for securing nuts, bolts or screws is: right is tight, left is loose. But if one seems stuck tight, sometimes turning it first a bit more to the right to dislodge rust will enable you to release it.

44 For very large nails, drill a pilot hole slightly smaller in diameter than the nail. This will reduce the possibility of splitting and make it easier to drive the nail in.

45 It may seem obvious, but you really should use brass screws for brass hinges, steel screws for steel hinges and black-lacquered painted screws for T-hinges.

46 Always use brass screws when working on oak, because steel ones will rust. But when using brass screws it is best first to insert a steel one of the same size, then to remove it and replace with brass. This will prevent your screwdriver damaging the softer brass screw.

47 Where possible use two hands to drive a screw, and use screw caps on thin materials to prevent splitting.

48   To tighten a loose screw, remove it, glue a wooden matchstick into the hole and screw it back again.

49   Cut pencil stubs into suitable lengths to make rawlplugs. The graphite in the pencil makes it easy for the hook or screw to enter the wood.

50   If you're nailing timber which has a tendency to split, nip off the point of the nails with a pair of pliers or pincers. This leaves a 'spade' end, which, if you position it straight across the grain, will stop the wood splintering.

51   If hinges and screws are to be painted, it's worth remembering that, should they ever need to be released, it's easier to remove paint from a slotted screw than from a crosshead screw.

52   For extra strength on a T-hinge – which is ideal for doors and garden gates etc. – use a nut and bolt in place of one of the screws on the hang flap.

53   Where a heavy load such as a garden gate has to be supported by hinges, using three rather than the conventional two will distribute the weight better.

54   Use rising butt hinges on internal house doors to allow clearance over carpets.

Sawing and Drilling

55   Saws will glide better if rubbed on both sides with the stub of an old candle. Apply pressure on the downward stroke.

Pointing your first finger down the saw will keep it balanced and give better control.

 When sawing plywood, stick masking tape along the line to be cut so as to prevent splintering.

 To end a cut without the waste breaking off and leaving a jagged end, support the waste with your other hand and use slow, careful strokes.

 When working with long pieces of timber, to prevent the cut closing up and jamming behind the saw, stick a piece of cardboard or a fine wooden wedge into the start once you get going.

 To stop a drill bit slipping on a smooth surface such as ceramic tiles or metal, cover the area with insulating or masking tape.

Stitching

61 Where the material is tough and the thread has to take the strain, waxed dental floss is a useful stand-by for sewing everything from buttons on overalls to toolbags and upholstery.

62 A crochet hook or eyebrow tweezers speed up the removal of tacking thread from upholstery, soft furnishings etc.

63 Use a see-through plastic toothbrush container to store upholstery needles and crochet hooks or eyebrow tweezers.

64 Dried up felt-tip pens are handy for cleaning fluff from awkward crevices in sewing machines.

65 A stretched sewing machine belt will tighten again if placed in cold water for half an hour and hung out in strong sunlight to dry.

See also 19.

Ladders

66 If you're investing in one all-purpose ladder, a wooden combination type is probably best. It can be used as a triple extension ladder, as simple steps, or can provide a scaffold when made into a pair of trestles to support a plank. Wood is heavier than aluminium, but you may feel more secure because of this.

67 Unstable ladders account for a large percentage of DIY accidents. The correct angle is 75° (one foot out for every four feet in height). Check your ladder for cracks, loose rungs etc. On soft ground, place a wide board under its feet. Never overreach.

 A ladder top must rest against a firm surface, so tie it in place if possible. Bind with cloth to prevent damage to paintwork.

 Never climb above the third rung from the top – i.e. you should never have more than your head and shoulders clear.

DIY Tools for the DIY Person

 Redundant skateboards or an old hot water bottle with the neck cut off and stuffed with old tights and rags make good kneeling pads for low-level DIY work.

71 If you don't own a spirit level, here's how you can improvise to get a pretty well accurate upright and level line when hanging shelves etc. Take a drawing pin and push it into the wall at eye level. Hang from it a long piece of stout cotton with a small weight – such as a washer – which will swing clear of the floor. Mark the wall at two places along the cotton, one above the other and reasonably close to each other. Take out the drawing pin, place a straight edge on the two marks and draw a line between them. To make a level horizontal line, take a sheet of paper (the larger this sheet the more accurate the end result will be) and fold it corner to corner. *See diagram.*

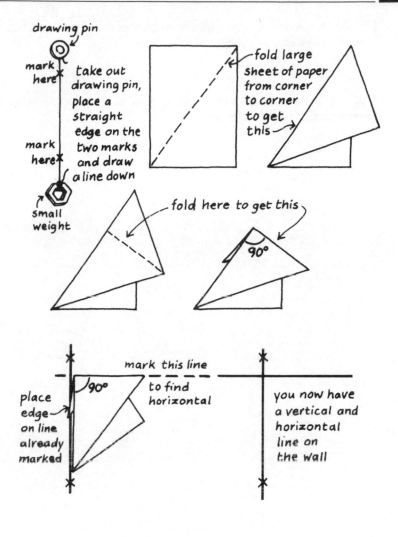

drawing pin

mark here — take out drawing pin, place a straight edge on the two marks and draw a line down

mark here

small weight

fold large sheet of paper from corner to corner to get this

fold here to get this

90°

place edge on line already marked

90°

mark this line to find horizontal

you now have a vertical and horizontal line on the wall

Cleaning Up

72   Baby oil or cold cream are handy stuff when applied on cotton wool to remove glue, putty, wet plaster and whatever else inevitably finds its way into your hair.

A canister of baby wipes is invaluable in or near a toolbox for a quick clean of hands and utensils.

74 Give the dustpan a coat of wax polish – the mess will glide off quickly to aid clearing up.

Home Maintenance: Structure and Fabric

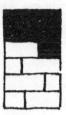

This chapter deals with the basics of looking after the actual building that is your home, along with its fixtures and fittings – the bits you leave behind when you sell up. Chapter 4 deals with the contents – the possessions that you take with you when you go. (Fitted carpets belong to houses rather than people and are generally negotiated with the purchase price and left behind. Looking after carpets in general, however, is covered in Chapter 4, laying them in Chapter 6.) Improving your home – adding to its value – is dealt with in Chapter 6. This section includes items such as fashionable decorative finishes for walls (as opposed to straightforward painting and papering), putting in a new fireplace and installing double glazing.

Decorating

○ *Preparation and making good . . .*

| 75 | Use a baby's bottle brush to shift the grime from in between radiator grids before painting. |

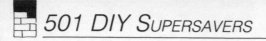

 Loosen any pipe joints or radiator valves before painting and smear Vaseline on them. They will tighten up easily when the paint dries.

 A cotton bud dipped in white shoe polish disguises the odd mark on walls before painting.

 To prepare walls for painting, always wash them from the bottom upwards to avoid streaking. Add a little paraffin to the bucket of soap suds to shift the dirt quicker. Rinse well from top to bottom.

 Clean dingy paintwork on windows with an old flannel or woolly sock dipped in paraffin. Remove with a clean cloth, and use the oily ones for firelighters later.

 Coving, the carved moulding which fits between ceiling and wall, can be bought in sections from DIY shops and will fill any gaps.

 Block awkward-shaped holes around pipes, wires and cables with foam polyurethane in aerosol cans.

○ *Plaster and putty . . .*

82 To cover a crack in a wall, use a piece of calico or white bandage and then paste well around the wall surface with wallpaper adhesive. Smooth the material over the hole. Once it's dry, it will tighten.

83 The point of a beer can opener is useful for cleaning out loose rubble before refilling cracks. Brush out remaining powdery bits before damping down and applying plaster (*see 87*).

84 Fill small holes in plaster with toothpaste, which will set hard and can be sanded down flush with the wall surface if necessary.

85 To fill a larger hole, reduce the gap as much as possible so that you only have the surface to plaster on. Crumpled chicken wire makes a good mesh on which to build a papier mâché casing. Soak paper and wallpaper paste until it resembles thick porridge. Add it layer by layer to the base and allow it several hours to set.

86 Very large areas in need of replastering are best left to a skilled tradesman. Plastering is 90% skill, 10% knowledge, but you can patch-plaster the professional way. Start at the top, feed in the plaster with an upward movement, and smooth level with a straight-edge. When firm, give a final wipe with a damp sponge to remove marks.

87 To replace a small detail of chipped moulding, make an impression from a sound section using plasticine. Lightly grease the inside and fill with plaster (or dentists' alginate – *see 311*). Use thinned down plaster as an adhesive to stick the replacement bit in place.

88 Here's how to plaster round chips in corners. Hold a wooden batten against one side of the corner. Fill the plaster up to the edge. Now hold the batten against the edge you've just filled and work into it. Smooth the edge with a wet, rubber-gloved finger.

89   To loosen stubborn putty, apply paint stripper and leave to soak for twenty minutes, or carefully heat the old putty with a hot poker. It will then come out easily.

90   Wrap left-over putty in kitchen foil and store it in the fridge, where it will keep in perfectly usable condition for up to a year.

○   *Brushes and rollers . . .*

 91   Before using a new brush, work the bristles back and forth in the palm of your hand to dislodge fibres or loose hairs.

92   Condition new paintbrushes by soaking them in linseed oil to give them a protective coat. Clean out the oil with white spirit before you start.

 93   A blob of hair conditioner added to the last rinse before putting brushes away keeps them supple in between jobs.

94 When soaking paintbrushes, clip a clothes peg to the handle so that the bristles don't rest on the bottom of the jar, which causes them to bend.

95 For a really thorough clean, suspend brushes in paraffin (cheaper than branded cleaners). The residue falls to the bottom of the jar, leaving on top a clear liquid which can be poured off and used again.

96 To hang up brushes for storage, attach ring pulls from drinks cans to the brush handles or else drill holes so that they can be hung up. Otherwise wrap them in several layers of newspaper or kitchen foil to protect the bristles.

97 Old brushes which have gone slightly hard will soften if the bristle part is boiled in vinegar. You'll need a cellulose thinner for solid ones.

98 Prepare a new roller by soaking it in soapy water for a few hours to release odd bits of fibre, which slow you down by spoiling the finish. Rinse and dry the roller thoroughly before using.

99 You will save up to a cupful of paint by scraping off a roller before washing it. Pop the leftovers into a small container for touch-up jobs later (*see 126*).

○ *Setting yourself up . . .*

100 An old shower cap is the most practical form of headgear when tackling overhead jobs such as painting or papering.

101 Don't wear anything woolly when painting – wandering fibres are drawn as if by a magnet to wet paint.

102 Instead of using an expensive air freshener, cut an onion in half and place it in a bowl of water to draw the smells from a room whilst you are painting it. Throw the onion away afterwards.

○ *Painting . . .*

103 It is false economy to buy cheap brands. They go on badly and you'll need more to get decent coverage. Buy the best makes and carefully thin down according to the manufacturer's instructions.

104 DIY superstores report surprisingly large numbers of complaints from irate customers who ruin the boot of their car with spills from tins of paint, varnish etc. Before driving off, make sure lids are wedged securely and properly protected in a double layer of plastic bags.

105 If you are uncertain about a new paint colour, buy test pots (available in leading brands) and paint round both sides of a corner to see how it looks in light and shade. The price of a sample pot should be refundable when you buy a larger quantity.

106 Stuck with a large quantity of paint that's too bright? Experiment with a small amount, adding some white, or – surprisingly, perhaps – a little black to tone down the colour.

107 Paint inside the can rarely matches the colour guide on the exterior, so paint the lid to show you more accurately what it looks like.

108 When you've finished, mark on the outside of the tin the level of paint left inside.

109 A high ceiling appears lower if painted in dark colours – reds, browns, blues or greens are particularly effective. White ceilings give the impression of height.

110 An attractive feature, such as a window, fireplace, door or alcove, will have twice the impact if painted white against a contrasting background.

111   To hide an unattractive feature in a room, paint it in the same colour as the wall so that it blends in.

112   Before painting, stand the paint tin upside down at room temperature for a few hours – it'll run better and go further. Stand enamel paint in a tin of hot water to thin it down naturally and get a porcelain-like finish.

113   It is hardly worth dirtying a roller tray for a small stretch of painting. Put the tray inside a plastic bag, which will mould itself to the tray when you pour the paint in. Secure the end firmly.

114   Before painting, pop yoghurt pots, slit up the side, on to handles and doorknobs and around light bulbs.

115   Stretch clingfilm over small tables to cover up vulnerable surfaces in a flash.

116   Professional decorators always decant paint from a tin to a paint kettle for easier use. Strain it through a nylon stocking or a pair of old tights to remove lumps of skin.

117   To prevent skin forming in the first place, store tightly shut paint tins upside down to form a seal.

118   To stop paint dripping down your arm when painting the ceiling, push the paintbrush handle through a small paper plate or an old sponge.

119   To catch drips from a paint tin, stand it on a paper plate or kitchen foil.

120 To prevent paint splashes on windowpanes, stick wet newspaper or clingfilm on to the glass.

121 A rim of Vaseline or washing up liquid keeps the line from straying when painting window frames, and protects small metal fittings.

122 Paint over light switches with luminous paint so that a child can locate them easily in the dark.

123 For best results when painting timber, always brush in the same direction as the wood grain.

124 Stopping for a short break during painting? Wrap an emulsion brush in clingfilm or in a cloth dampened in water to stop it drying out. For oil-based paint, use white spirit on the cloth.

125 Tie a string across the rim of a paint or paste kettle, to wipe off surplus paint and rest the brush when you take a break.

126 Baby food jars make ideal containers for patch-up amounts of paint or leftover wallpaper paste to be used when necessary later.

See also 341–358.

○ *Wallpapering . . .*

 Cheap wallpaper tears and wrinkles easily. Buy the best you can afford.

 Using dress or curtain material on walls instead of paint or wallpaper can work out cheaper, with fewer draughts and a cosier look. Put up wooden battens and then attach the cloth to them with a staple gun. For even more warmth and less noise, insert polyester padding between the battens before attaching the fabric. *See also 361–368.*

 Grease spots on wallpaper can often be removed by placing a piece of blotting paper on top of the stain and ironing over it.

130 For easy wallpaper stripping, soak the walls well with warm soapy water rather than pricey, proprietary brands of stripper.

131 To remove stubborn patches of old emulsion paint, paint over it with cellulose wallpaper paste and leave for ten minutes before removing it.

 Before hanging paper, apply a coat of wallpaper paste around any crack which is wider than hairline and smooth a strip of white bandage over the opening to conceal it.

133 Lining paper is cheap, improves the look of less-than-perfect walls and acts as a base for paint too. Used under wallpaper, it should be pasted on horizontally (known as cross lining) to prevent any seam coming in the same place as a seam on the covering paper.

134 Leftover lining paper from an unfinished roll makes inexpensive drawer liners (*see also 141*).

135 A stick of paper adhesive (Pritt Stick) is handy for gluing down dried out bits of ready-pasted wallpaper if there isn't any paste left to do the job.

136 When working behind radiators paste the wall and not the paper, and guide the paper down with a padded coathanger or long-handled roller.

137 If picture pins and screws on walls are to be used again, before papering take them out and insert matchsticks in the walls where they've been. The matches will pop through the damp wallpaper, marking the position. *See also 317.*

138 If paper keeps rolling back on itself on the pasting table, secure a piece of elastic across the table with drawing pins and slide the paper under it.

139 If your wallpaper seems stiff and unworkable, let the paste soak in for between two and fifteen minutes. Soak each length for the same time, to give a uniform stretch throughout.

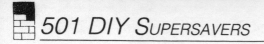

140 Leave bubbles in wallpaper for twenty-four hours. If they haven't flattened themselves by then, prick them with a sharp knife and, with the aid of a cocktail stick or cotton bud, stick some adhesive inside the cut and smooth it down with your fingers.

141 Store spare rolls of wallpaper in old stockings or tights and use odd pieces for lining drawers. These pieces will gradually fade along with that on the walls and will therefore be perfect for patching. For an instant faded look, coat with lemon juice.

Floors

○ *Getting up the old . . .*

142 To remove a damaged floor tile, place a sheet of aluminium foil over it and iron on top of that to soften the adhesive. Once warmed, the centre can be pierced with a sharp knife and the unwanted material easily lifted off.

|143| To remove glued-on sheet floor coverings such as linoleum or vinyl, a sharp-edged garden spade is as useful a tool as any to get underneath them without straining your back.

○ *Preparation and making good . . .*

|144| Silence squeaky floorboards or stairs with a good shake of talcum powder in the joists or gaps between them.

|145| Narrow gaps between floorboards can be quickly sealed with strips of draught excluder. Fill larger ones with papier mâché (*see 86*).

|146| Block off gaps between skirting and floorboards with an acrylic emulsion-type sealant or with timber beading secured to the floor with panel pins.

|147| For a cheap gap-stopper get a packet of wallpaper paste, mix it to the consistency of thick porridge, soak strips of brown paper in it and build it up layer by layer.

Hardboard fixed to floorboards eliminates draughts and is usually necessary before laying sheet vinyl or tiles.

○ *Putting down the new . . .*

 Cork tiles are warmer than vinyl, cheaper and just as durable. Easy to lay, untreated cork can be sealed for easy cleaning.

150 Quick-setting adhesives are usually necessary for laying floor tiles in busy areas such as kitchens which can't be turned into no-go areas for long. The alternative is to tile in sections, not walking on newly laid tiles for at least twenty-four hours.

 Before laying linoleum or vinyl, leave it in a heated room or in the sun all day so that the warmth penetrates the centre of the roll, making it more pliable and therefore less likely to crack.

152 Cut vinyl generously as it is apt to shrink.

 Environment-friendly linoleum is making a comeback – don't tack it down for a day or two to allow it to 'tread out' and prevent bulges, as it is inclined to stretch.

 When cutting linoleum to shape for awkward curves and corners, bend thin wire – an uncurled coat hanger will do – into the required shape. Place it on the linoleum and cut round it.

○ *Cleaning . . .*

Clean up dingy linoleum and vinyl by adding paraffin to the water. It will shift the dirt and add a shine without making the surface dangerously slippery.

Remove cement from floor tiles by rubbing them with linseed oil.

157 Soapy water should never be used on stone floors, it can make them extremely slippery. Stubborn grease marks will dissolve in a special cleaner for garage floors which is available from car accessory shops.

For carpets see 218–233, 329–335.

Wall Tiles

158 If you're tired of your existing wall tiles, try to avoid removing them because you'll probably damage the wall surface. Paint over them – or better still, provided that they are not cracked, just lay new tiles on top.

159 It's essential to use waterproof adhesive for tiles near areas which will get wet through splashes or condensation – wash-basin surrounds and shower stalls, for example.

When buying tiles always include a few spare to replace those that get damaged during fixing or use. Buying them later isn't as good – a different batch may alter in colour and thickness.

 To remove a broken tile, cover it with a cross of masking tape before using a chisel to prise it out.

 When the grouting in between tiles has become stained or discoloured, clean it with household bleach on a toothbrush.

 White tiles are cheapest, but you may think too clinical. Framing them with brightly coloured grout puts them in the designer bracket. Alternatively stencil on them.

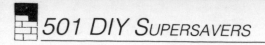 Clean grubby ceramic tiles with a half-and-half mix of linseed oil and turps, shaken up in a screw-top jar. If painting over the tiles, however, give them a scrub with sugar soap to help the paint adhere to the shiny surface.

Hanging Pictures

If you haven't got proper picture pins and are using nails, to stop the plaster cracking when hanging a picture, place Sellotape on the desired spot before driving your nail into the wall. *See also 317–318.*

Baths, Sinks and Washbasins

 Treat stains on enamel baths by rubbing in salt on a soft cloth dampened in white spirit, vinegar or paraffin. Slight scratches may be gently removed with metal polish.

167 Gaps between sinks and walls, tiles and baths etc. should be sealed with flexible waterproof sealant.

168 To give flexible sealant round a bath or washbasin twice the sticking power, use a hairdryer to remove every trace of moisture from the surrounds before applying. Don't use the bath for twenty-four hours afterwards.

169 Bring mouldy shower curtains back to their sparkling best by soaking them in water containing half a cup of bleach and a quarter cup of detergent. After twenty minutes they should be ready to rinse and drip dry.

170 Rusty steel reacts brilliantly to a rub from a cut onion. Really work it into the stain and leave the coating of juice for a couple of days before polishing with turpentine and washing off.

171 If a steel sink is looking the worse for wear, scour it out with a little turpentine on a piece of rough towelling. Then rinse thoroughly and polish up with a soft rag.

172 Remove corrosion around chrome taps and fittings with paraffin or damp bicarbonate of soda. Use a toothbrush to get into the nooks and crannies.

173 For an economical chrome cleaner, use paraffin applied with a soft cloth, bicarbonate of soda on a soft damp cloth, or washing soda diluted in water.

174 Stop rust developing on chrome by rubbing a thin coat of Vaseline over the surface.

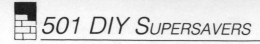

Doors and Windows

175 To save straining your back, use leverage techniques when hanging a door: to hold it in place while you secure the hinges, push a garden spade underneath and press down on the handle to shift the load. *See also 35.*

○ *Getting things working . . .*

176 If a bolt refuses to budge, a dousing from a can of Coca Cola or a few drops of ammonia left to soak in for a couple of seconds should make it unstick.

177 Locks won't jam if powdered graphite is puffed into the mechanism. (It also stops piano pedals squeaking.) Don't use oil – it attracts dirt and will eventually make the problem worse.

178 A door which is slightly sticking at the bottom can have the offending bit sanded off by pulling it backwards and forwards over a sheet of coarse glasspaper until it moves freely.

179 If a door is sticking at the side, rub some chalk down the edge where it meets the frame, and then close it. When the door is opened again, the frame will be marked at the sticking place. Rub it down with sandpaper.

180 Sliding doors and drawers will glide more easily with moist soap or candlewax rubbed along the runners.

181 If a wooden door knob comes loose and won't fit the hole again because the thread has worn, glue round the shaft and wrap a layer of material round it to pad out the opening.

|182| Rub a creaking hinge with Vaseline, a lead pencil or washing up liquid.

|183| Those fiddly brass bits that you remove when stripping wooden doors and furniture can be popped in a dip of boiled haricot bean water to restore their sparkle. *See also 286, 288–291.*

○ *Window wisdom . . .*

|184| Make sash windows burglarproof – drill a hole in both outer and inner window frames and insert a sash or dual screw. Drill a second hole part of the way up the upper window and the window can be bolted even when partially open to let air in.

|185| Soap sash cords on windows for easier opening.

|186| A crack in a leaded window can often be disguised by turning it into a 'stained' glass feature, using a simple coloured glass kit from DIY shops. *See also 360.*

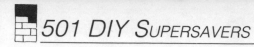

187 Remove a cracked pane of glass by covering it with adhesive tape and breaking it with a hammer.

o *Cleaning windows . . .*

188 It speeds up window cleaning if you dry one side of the pane horizontally and on the other use vertical strokes. Stubborn smears will show up quite easily.

189 Never throw money away on expensive branded window cleaning fluids. Instead toss crumpled newspaper into a bowl of tepid water containing a good dash of ammonia, methylated spirit or vinegar, and polish off with dry newspapers. The final sparkle lies in the printers' ink.

o *Bright ideas . . .*

190 Cotton reels make super doorstops. Secure them to the floor with long screws and paint to blend with the decor.

Gas

191 Leave gas plumbing to experts, and take care when using a blowtorch in combined spaces or near combustible material. Not so long ago a man working with a blowlamp to remove paint from his garage set fire to the roofs of a whole row of terraced houses in Norwich.

Fires and Fireplaces

○ *Cleaning and maintenance . . .*

192 To clean a gas fire which has been discoloured by smoke, sprinkle it liberally with salt when cold. When the fire is next lit, the salt and stain will burn off together.

193 The best time to have a chimney swept is in early spring, before spring cleaning or redecorating. If the fire is to remain unused for some time, fit a plasterboard or plywood backdrop for shade-loving plants. Cut it out to fit the opening, and paint it black or a colour to match the room. The board will stop draughts as well as cutting down dust and grime from the chimney.

194 Potato peelings burnt on the fire not only help it to burn more easily, but stop soot forming.

195   Extinguish a chimney fire quickly by pouring lots of kitchen salt on the flames, or carefully damp it with water. The rising steam will put out flames in the flue.

196   Cut out the expense of commercial flue cleaners and make your own mix from 1lb (450g) of flowers of sulphur and 8oz (225g) of saltpetre. When the fire is burning bright and clear, throw a handful on to the fire to slacken the soot and remove the build-up.

○   *Renovation . . .*

197   Renovate cast-iron fireplaces with a coat of black stove enamel.

198   Use a rustproof product such as Hammerite on dingy metal surrounds and accessories.

199   A quick-setting, heatproof cement is particularly suitable around loose marble or stonework.

200   Make use of a free guide for amateur fireplace restorers – *Opening Up Your Fireplace*, obtainable from the Solid Fuel Advisory Service, who also supply colour brochures of the various models manufactured and distributed by their members. Look in Yellow Pages for your local SFAS office, or dial 100 and ask for Freefone Real Fires.

See also 328.

Bright Ideas

201   If you can't afford to replace ugly old radiators, or don't like the look of them anyway, hide them with an attractive casing of brass builders' mesh, painted trellis or even fine mesh chicken wire pulled taut on to a frame.

202 Garden trellis can be painted white and attached to a not-so-perfect wall surface for a summery look, saving a plasterer's bill.

Exteriors

203 To remove splashes of cement, dirty marks or paint drips from bricks, use another brick, in the manner of an eraser, to rub it off.

204 When fixing trellis to an outside wall, first mark where the corners will go. Drill at these points and attach cotton reels, then fix the trellis to them.

205 When laying concrete, most people know to stop it drying out quickly in very hot weather by spraying with water, but just as harmful in cold conditions is frost. If frost is forecast, and you have recently laid concrete, cover the protective sheet with sand, earth or straw which can be anchored by putting another sheet and bricks on top.

206 Cracks in paving stones can be opened, cleaned and filled with cement. Alternatively lift out the damaged one and replace it. If they are all badly cracked, get a sledgehammer, smash the whole lot and fill with cement mix for instant crazy paving.

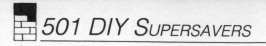

207 Rusted wrought iron gates, weathervanes or whatever can be cleaned with paraffin applied on fine wire wool. Once cleaned, shine the metal up with a coat of furniture polish. But if the surface is badly pitted, restore it with a rustproof metal paint such as Hammerite.

Home Maintenance: Contents

Curtains and Blinds

○ *Cleaning and maintenance . . .*

|208| Put dirty curtain rings and runners into a bowl containing two parts hot water to one of vinegar, and let them soak for a few hours before rubbing them dry with rough towelling.

|209| To help rods slide freely through blinds or curtains, slip a thimble or a finger from an old rubber glove (inside out) over the end.

210 Using silicone furniture polish on metal curtain rods will ensure that the runners move freely.

211 To clean a washable roller blind, unroll it bit by bit over the edge of the bath and scrub with a nailbrush and mild detergent dissolved in barely warm water. If there is a danger that washing might shrink it, dry clean by rubbing it with flour or oatmeal on a piece of clean towelling.

212 Venetian blinds can be dry cleaned using an L-shaped chunk of crusty bread. Slip an old sock over your hand and dip in a soapy solution for ones that can be washed.

213 If a blind snaps in place too rapidly, remove and unroll half way down by hand, then replace on the brackets. If it won't catch once pulled down, remove the blind and check that the brackets haven't been damaged. Adjust with pliers if necesary and oil the mechanism, wiping away any surplus to avoid getting it on the fabric. Replace the blind and try again.

o *Choosing and making . . .*

 Where curtains exist on a small window, the window will look bigger if the pole or track is a good bit wider than the recess. The curtains will then hang well to each side of the frame or can be tied back with a cord.

`215` A small room will look less cluttered if a blind rather than a curtain is used.

`216` A simple lace blind could be the answer to a tiny window. Don't hem it at the bottom. Instead just attach it to the top rod and cut the bottom following the shape of the pattern, to allow it to hang free.

`217` Cut out curtain material on a rectangular table, lining up the selvedge so that it runs exactly down the longer side. Chalk a mark where it bends over the edge, and cut along this line.

See also 464.

Carpets

o *Wear and tear, spills and stains . . .*

`218` Disguise a badly worn cord runner by laying a strip of brightly coloured canvas down the middle to cover threadbare patches.

`219` Remove charred carpet fibres, caused by cigarette burns or sparks from the fire, by rubbing over with fine sandpaper. Then rub with a piece of towelling dipped in a mild detergent solution. Rinse and dry thoroughly.

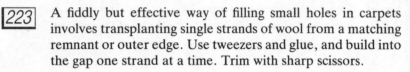

220 Hold frayed edges on rugs and carpets in check with a latex adhesive such as Copydex. Brush it halfway up the tufts, and when dry it will hold the edge neatly in line.

221 On carpets where the backing is showing, try a strong solution of dye matching the most prominent colour. Apply to the worn parts with a toothbrush.

222 To disguise small worn areas or scorch marks, colour the threads with felt tip pens in appropriate colours.

223 A fiddly but effective way of filling small holes in carpets involves transplanting single strands of wool from a matching remnant or outer edge. Use tweezers and glue, and build into the gap one strand at a time. Trim with sharp scissors.

224 Enhance the colour of faded carpets with a solution of 1 part vinegar to 3 parts boiling water, rubbed on with clean, well wrung-out cloths.

225 A dent in a carpet will rise again if an ice cube is left overnight on the spot. To raise the pile, next day iron the area over a cloth until the carpet is bone dry.

226   Here's a solution for big holes or indelible stains. Cut a square around the damaged part using a Stanley knife. Use this piece as a template to get a matching square from a remnant. Turn the carpet over and fix a larger square of canvas on the underside with Latex adhesive. Allow to dry. Now turn the carpet back – right side up – and glue the underside of the new patch, which can then be fitted neatly into the space.

227   Fresh wax, oil or grease stains on carpets can be removed if you iron through blotting paper and rub off with turpentine on a clean rag.

228   Treat ink or soot spills immediately, by pouring on a generous pile of salt. As it absorbs, remove the surplus with a knife or teaspoon. Repeat the process if necessary, finally rubbing over the mark with a cut lemon.

229   For paint spills on carpets or other soft furnishings, scrape off the surplus immediately and treat according to paint type. Sponge emulsion with cold water, working from the edge to the centre of the spill. Gloss or other oil-based paint needs white spirit, carbon tetrachloride, or a proprietary dry cleaning solution such as Thawpit or Dabitoff. With acrylic paints, soak off as much as possible with soft tissues before applying methylated spirit or dry cleaning solvent.

230   Once dried, emulsion paint is virtually impossible to remove, but you'll get the best advice from the Carpet Cleaners' Association, 126 New Walk, Leicester, LE1 7JA (tel. 0533–554352).

See also 264–276, 392.

For laying carpets see 329–335.

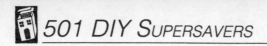
○ *Small rugs . . .*

 Make rugs non-slip on polished floors by sewing rubber rings from jam jars, at the corners. Alternatively use strips from bicycle inner tubes or from old hot water bottles.

 Stop rug corners curling by sewing at each corner triangular pockets containing lead weights (obtainable from hardware shops).

 Give new, white-fringed oriental rugs an antique look by carefully sponging the fringes with cold tea.

Furniture

○ *Dealing with damage . . .*

 Dents in stripped furniture rise again if you leave a damp cloth on them overnight and iron over it the next day.

 Scratches in furniture will certainly improve, and probably disappear, if treated with cod liver oil. Leave for twenty-four hours before polishing off.

 You can often fill in scratches – even tiny cracks – on a wooden surface with a child's wax crayon in a matching colour. Rub until it's flush with the surface, and then use beeswax polish to blend it in.

 The traditional way to treat water and alcohol stains on polished surfaces is with a mixture of cigarette ash and castor oil. Treat heat stains with spirit of camphor or camphorated oil.

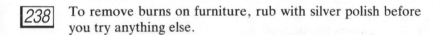

238   To remove burns on furniture, rub with silver polish before you try anything else.

239   For white rings on French-polished furniture, cigar ash mixed with olive oil works best. Rub light woods with a Brazil nut.

240   White rings on other furniture finishes respond to a vigorous rubbing with toothpaste, or a mixture of salad oil and salt, or a dab of mayonnaise, or Brasso.

241   Treat white heat marks on a varnished surface with a half-and-half mix of linseed oil and methylated spirits.

242   Veneer finishes react favourably to salt and olive oil mixed to a paste and left to soak in overnight. But first try the cut surface of a brazil nut if you have one handy.

243 Periodically rub garden furniture with linseed oil to prevent cracks and splits.

244 To stop a table leg wobbling, mix wood shavings with wood glue and put some of the mixture under the offending leg. When the glue is well set, trim away the excess.

245 Use white of egg to glue on chips from a veneered surface. (Egg white is also useful for repairing torn pages of books.)

○ *Polishing and renovation . . .*

246 Frugal furniture polish needs only melted candle stubs, odd bits of soap, turpentine and linseed oil. Take two household candles or the equivalent in stubs, plus 8oz (225g) leftover soap melted in ¾ cup of boiling water. Mix thoroughly and allow to cool. Now add ¼ cup turpentine and ¼ cup linseed oil, mix well and decant into a screw-top jar. Always shake well before use.

247 Beeswax comes in two varieties, yellow and bleached – the latter being for light wood. Make your own polish by grating 14oz (395g) beeswax into 32 fl oz (800ml) turpentine, and leaving in a jar overnight. The following day thoroughly shake the mixture, stand the container in a bowl of hot water and stir until it forms a paste.

248 To recondition cheap junkshop furniture, coat it with linseed oil and leave it for a week to feed the wood. Add a shine with beeswax polish. *See also 320, 389, 391.*

To renovate old or neglected leather-covered furniture, put two parts linseed oil and one part white vinegar in a screw-top jar and shake to mix. Apply with a soft cloth. Alternatively use a mixture of equal parts turps, methylated spirit, vinegar and paraffin. *See also 309.*

 Surgical spirit carefully sponged on to leather upholstery will remove grease stains. When dry, go over the whole piece with wax polish.

 Secondhand cane furniture goes for a song when it becomes baggy. Sponge the whole piece with warm salt water. Turn it upside down, pour really hot water all over it and dry it in the sun. The cane will shrink and tighten.

252 For an antique wicker look, buy new but cheap wicker furniture and cover it with several thin coats of clear varnish. Alternatively use a rich brown varnish over linseed oil mixed with artists' oil paint.

For restoring old beams see 359.

Upholstery

○ *Cleaning and repair . . .*

253 The colour of Dralon upholstery perks up considerably if lightly rubbed with a white vinegar and warm water solution applied on a well wrung-out chamois.

 For an emergency upholstery cleaner, you can't beat a squirt of shaving foam. Wipe over with a well wrung-out cloth containing a hint of vinegar.

 When repairing upholstery use a curved needle designed for the job, and knot each thread end separately to avoid tangles.

 Repair zip fasteners on loose covers etc. by pulling the slide down to just below the broken teeth. Cut out the damaged part. Pull the slide carefully and evenly, engaging the teeth on two sides. Once past the broken bit, make a new base by firmly stitching across it.

Old zips on loose covers will come up like new if sprayed with starch before the cover is ironed.

 Sticky zips need a rub with a lead pencil to help them glide more easily.

○ *Doing your own upholstery . . .*

259 When buying material for loose or fitted covers, get enough extra to make arm protectors and head rests. These are the areas where the material wears out first and gets dirty.

260 Invest in a power staple gun if you are undertaking a fair amount of upholstery work. It makes fitting underlay, or fixing fabric around sofas, a doddle. An electric one, preferably with an adjustable punch, does all the work for you, stapling various materials from paper to plywood.

261 When re-covering furniture, use the old material as a pattern to cut from. Mark and steam-press the material first, along the line where it is to be turned under.

○ *Cushions . . .*

262 Decent-sized, well-filled cushions are expensive. Make your own from feather pillows bought in the sale. Shake them until the filling drops into a square at one end. Cut off the surplus and re-sew or fix with Velcro.

263 An even cheaper cushion filling can be made by saving old woolly jumpers or buying them in jumble sales. Wash and dry them well, unravel the wool and chop it up into a springy filling. For extra filling you can add chopped tights or stockings.

Dirt and Stains on Fabrics and Upholstery

264 Always test the colour fastness of fabrics by wetting a corner and ironing it between two pieces of white cloth.

If you have trouble identifying a stain, start by applying a paste of Fuller's earth and cold water and cover the mark with this. Brush off when it's dry. It won't harm non-fast-coloured materials.

 To clean delicate rugs, blinds or fabrics where the colour may run, use potato water. Grate two potatoes and add to a pint of water in a basin. Let it soak for a while, stirring from time to time. Strain it through a sieve into a pint of fresh water. Stir, and when settled decant the clear part into a bottle. Apply it carefully with a sponge, and rinse off with cold water.

 Remove paint stains with hot vinegar.

 Wet grass stains with cold water, cover with cream of tartar (available from chemists), and where possible bleach dry in hot sunlight.

 Tar, bitumen or pitch stains and machine oil can usually be removed by first covering them with lard or margarine. Afterwards wash them first of all in lukewarm and then in hot soapy water, or rub with benzine (lighter fuel) on a clean cloth.

 For tar marks, try soaking a piece of white rag in eucalyptus oil and rubbing on the affected part until quite clean.

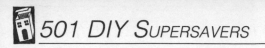 Wine stains promptly treated with a squirt from a soda syphon won't leave even a water mark.

Red wine stains can be removed with white wine, but a liberal sprinkling of salt to soak up the stain is cheaper and just as effective.

 Grease-stained fabric can be left overnight in a pre-soak biological wonder solution of tepid water and Coca Cola.

 Treat a scorch mark immediately by soaking it in cold milk.

275 To clean up dusty hessian, use the small attachment of a vacuum cleaner to draw surface dirt, then bring up the colour with a barely damp sponge which has been dipped in a vinegar and water solution.

276 Dirty modern tapestry and needlepoint need Fuller's earth, French chalk or warm bran worked into them, using a clean cloth or your fingertips. Leave it overnight before brushing out. Antique and fragile pieces need expert care. Museums can usually recommend specialists.

See also 227–230.

Household Cleaning and Repairs: General

 Brasso is a useful mild abrasive for the handy person. Use it to remove slight scratches on car paint and clock (or watch) faces.

○ *China and glass . . .*

 When gluing broken china, first grease lightly round the edges to stop stray glue setting as it oozes from the join. Wipe away the excess with a damp cloth.

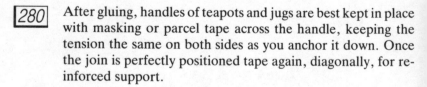 Many an object can be held together by clamping it in a drawer until the glue dries, but a box of sand is the ideal support for disabled china.

 After gluing, handles of teapots and jugs are best kept in place with masking or parcel tape across the handle, keeping the tension the same on both sides as you anchor it down. Once the join is perfectly positioned tape again, diagonally, for reinforced support.

 Small rubber bands will hold a broken thin-stemmed vase until the glue dries. Use a larger one round a damaged cup rim.

282 A small chip in a glass needn't mean that it has to be thrown out. Use the finest-grained wet-and-dry glasspaper and work it over the rim until smooth.

283 If the stem of a glass is broken, rest the bowl upside down on a flat surface. Fix a piece of plasticine or Blue-Tac on the bowl near the broken area and apply a suitable glass adhesive to both damaged surfaces. Press together, and push the plasticine against the join to support it. Take care not to wrap the support all round, which would obliterate the light which is essential to the bonding process.

284 There are countless tips for cleaning a glass decanter. One of the safest is to break eggshells in tiny pieces and place them in the vessel, adding a pinch of bicarbonate of soda and filling up with warm water. Shake well. Next day remove the contents and wash with warm soapy water. Add a dash of vinegar to the final rinsing water.

285 When a stopper won't budge inside a glass decanter, tap it very gently with another glass stopper. Try this 'like with like' method on flowerpots, stacked cups, pots and pans etc.

See also 490.

○ *Dirty and damaged metal . . .*

286 Soak grease or grime from brass or copper with a hot vinegar and salt solution. Shift verdigris with neat household ammonia and salt.

287 Another answer for soiled copper is a cut lemon or lime covered in salt and rubbed vigorously on the surface. Leave the juice to work for a few hours, then wash it off. When dry, polish with non-silicone furniture polish.

288 To clean up a really filthy brass, copper or unrecognizable metal object, coat it with a paste of equal parts flour, salt and vinegar. Leave overnight and wash off the next day.

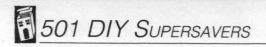

 Too busy to clean brass? The answer is to scrub the newly polished metal with hot water containing washing up liquid. Dry it with a soft cloth and then apply a coat of clear, acrylic metal lacquer.

 Without a protective coating, brass will stay tarnish-free longest when rubbed over with a cut, ripe tomato.

 To remove lacquer from brass, rub it with surgical spirit – don't use paint stripper.

 Silver stained with mildew can be cleaned with paraffin or a cut lemon, unless it has eaten right into the surface.

 Don't mistake dingy pewter for neglected silverware. Silver polishes don't do pewter any good at all. Polish it up with a cabbage leaf and keep it clean by washing regularly in a soapy water solution.

 Heavily corroded pewter should be immersed in a paraffin bath for a couple of days, then wiped over with a soft cloth dipped in methylated spirit and finally washed in warm soapy water. Rinse and dry thoroughly.

 The quickest way to clean encrusted dirt from grills, while they're still warm, is with mayonnaise applied on a wad of paper towels.

See also 183.

O   *Odds and ends . . .*

If fridges, washing machines and other kitchen appliances are shabby but in good working order, spruce up their bodywork with bath enamel. Alternatively stick masking tape on handles, hinges etc., put wedges of newspaper underneath, and apply car paint from a spray can in any colour you fancy. (Don't use these methods on cookers – only proper baked-on enamel will withstand this sort of heat.)

Typists' white correcting fluid disguises scratches on white paint, laminate, fridges and other enamelled surfaces.

Soap or detergents can discolour marble. Apply a mixture of one part powdered pumice, one part chalk and two parts bicarbonate of soda with enough water to form a thin paste. Brush it on to the surface, leave for twenty-four hours, then sponge off with plain water. Repolish if necessary, with whiting applied on a chamois leather.

Methylated spirit is the stuff for cleaning stained onyx.

Attach small pieces of sponge where the bedsprings and slats meet, and you'll put an end to irritating squeaks.

If you are using metal clamps when repairing wooden objects, strips cut from old rubber inner tubes come in handy for protecting the wood.

Loose joints, loose broom and rake handles, may need some packing to make them tighter. Matches, cocktail sticks or ends of wooden clothes pegs make instant wedges. Wrap some thread round them before gluing the joint in place.

 Many a clock which has apparently ticked for the last time has miraculously lived to count another day after being placed in a barely warm oven to unclog the mechanism.

'AT THE FIRST STROKE...'

 A sticky or scratched iron can be cured if a tablet of soap is wrapped in a handkerchief and rubbed on the hot face of the iron.

 Unclog a steam iron with white vinegar poured in while the iron is still warm and left to sit in it until the sediment dissolves. Rinse well, using only rainwater, distilled water or still mineral water, to prevent a build-up of scale in future.

306 It needs only a few glass marbles or a clean oyster shell placed in the bottom of a kettle to prevent the build-up of scale.

307 Don't leave water in a jug kettle overnight – swill it out and stand it upside down on a tea-towel to cut down the build-up of scale.

Books

308 Treat bookbindings which are spotted with mould by rubbing in oil of lavender. This not only cleans them, but protects them from a recurrence of the mould problem.

309 Restore dried out leather bindings by rubbing on a mixture made from equal quantities of milk and egg white, beaten together and rubbed gently into the leather on a soft flannel. Polish up with an old silk handkerchief. *See also 249*.

Pictures and Mirrors

310 You can safely clean an oil painting by rubbing the surface with juice squeezed from a grated potato. Apply with a soft cloth in a circular movement. Alternatively rub gently with the juicy side of a cut onion.

311 To repair plaster mouldings on picture frames use alginate, a dental impression compound obtainable from dental suppliers or your friendly neighbourhood dentist who orders it in bulk.

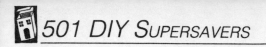

 Plastic wood putty will fill cracks and holes in wooden frames.

 Restore gilt picture frames with a mix of one beaten egg white to one teaspoon of bicarbonate of soda. Apply with a pastry brush and leave for a few minutes, then wipe off with neat washing up liquid.

 Make a picture frame look expensive by matching the frame to the predominant picture colour. Rubbing artists' oil paint into unattractive wood can add life to it.

 A metallic paint such as liquid leaf, applied over a primer on bare wooden frames, gives an antique look.

Restore the sparkle to grimy picture glass with a soft rag dipped in paraffin or methylated spirit. Then polish off with crumpled newspaper.

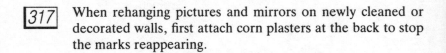

When rehanging pictures and mirrors on newly cleaned or decorated walls, first attach corn plasters at the back to stop the marks reappearing.

 When hanging mirrors treat them as if they were pictures, aligning the bigger ones to the tops of doors and using two picture hooks to hang them.

See also 165.

Bright Ideas

319   A large slab of cheap mirror glass becomes somewhat grand in a frame made from boards and secured to the wall with finishing nails, which have no heads. Cover with silk or sackcloth, brocade or PVC to suit your style or pocket.

320   Round glass tops over circular cloths disguise junkshop tables with startling effect. Be sure the edges of the glass are rounded and polished, and add a quilted lining as an underfelt beneath the cloth.

Improving Your Home

Insulation and
Double Glazing

321. It pays to plan ahead when buying insulating materials – bargains are to be found in the summer months when demand is lower.

322. Double glazing, installed by a reputable firm, can reduce heat loss by as much as 50%. With DIY double glazing a plastic channel is fitted. A pane of glass slides into it and is secured with special clips attached to the windowpanes.

See also 361–368, 370–380, 467–483.

Kitchen Planning and Storage

323 Doing your own kitchen planning? Copy professional designers who fit everything round an essential triangle – food storage, food preparation and cooking areas – to save walking time and to reduce the risk of accidents.

324 Shelves at eye level can be made to do double the work if you attach the lids of screw-top glass jars securely to the undersides. Fill the jars with odds and ends and screw them into the lids.

325 Small, trough-like shelves on the back of cupboard doors store fiddly things like herb jars, mustard pots, aluminium foil and clingfilm.

326 Attach two empty cotton reels in a cupboard just close enough for a broom head to sit on them and its handle to hang in between.

327 Cut spare curtain track into pieces the depth of a drawer. Then secure it inside at appropriate intervals to enable plywood dividers to be slotted in.

Installing a Fireplace

328 Although not an easy task for DIY enthusiasts, you may be able to do part of the work under the guidance of a fireplace restorer, thus cutting down labour costs. Find them in classified sections of magazines such as *Traditional Homes*. *See also 197–200.*

Laying Carpets

 Apportion funds available for carpets by investing in top-quality, harder-wearing carpets for hallways, stairs and sitting rooms, where wear and tear is greatest. In bedrooms you can get by with a cheaper kind.

 Invest in a good felt underlay to seal off cold underfloor air. Building paper or even newspapers are the pauper's alternatives. In between is paper underlay from carpet shops. Use double-sided carpet tape to fix underlay to a solid floor.

 The best way to measure for a stair carpet is with a string on the outside edge. Measure for the underlay separately.

332 A runner is cheaper than a wall-to-wall stair carpet, and it's easy to lay by yourself. Add 18 inches (45cm) extra when buying, so that you can fold the top and bottom under until you need to adjust the risers to replace worn treads.

333 If tackling carpet laying for the first time try a smaller area, such as a bathroom. Measure carefully and make paper patterns before cutting. Always keep remnants for repair jobs later.

334 Where central heating pipes run under the floor, gripper strip must always be stuck down and not nailed. If in doubt, turn the heating on full and walk the floor in bare feet.

335 To lay a carpet flush to the edges without leaving a gap between it and the skirting board, push the point of the blade against the bottom of the skirting, and holding the knife at an angle to the wall, push well in.

For care and maintenance of carpets see 218–230.

Putting Up Shelves

336 If you buy 'prepared timber' it is measured from the size it was before it was planed down. A piece of timber described as 2 × 1 inches (5 × 2.5cm) will therefore actually measure 1¾ × ¾ inches (4.25 × 1.75cm).

337 When measuring for shelves, remember not only the height of objects but also access to them. Will you need to pull out a plug behind a lamp, adjust a TV aerial, lift the lid of the record player or store surplus cable etc? Include the thickness of the shelves, too, in your calculations.

338 Never underestimate the weight a shelf will have to take. As a rule of thumb, a support every 30 inches (75cm) is needed along the length, but increase the number of brackets for heavy loads – books, records etc. – to prevent bowing.

339   Brackets should be 1 inch (2.5cm) less deep than the shelf depth. Check that there are no pipes, electric wires or cables running behind. Use 1½ inch (3.75cm) screws, brass preferably, and plug the walls first.

340   Don't rest timber on newspaper – the print can be absorbed into the grain, causing permanent discoloration.

Decorative Paint Finishes

○   *The basic idea . . .*

341   Transform blemished or plain furniture into a feature of the room with attractive stencil work on drawers, wardrobes, doors, cupboards etc. Stencil the floor or walls around attractive doors or pieces of furniture such as antique chests, to highlight them.

342   Old-fashioned lavatory cisterns become works of art when painted and stencilled. Complete the picture by adding a length of stout curtain cord with a tassel on the end, rather than a tacky chrome chain.

343   Experiment with textures and patterns. When there was a shortage of wallpaper in the twenties, enterprising homemakers scrunched torn up pieces of muslin or lace with which to 'rag' their walls. Homemakers of the nineties use J-cloths, plastic bags, crumpled white tissue paper and even old chamois leathers for interesting results.

344 The effects of decorative painting will be spoiled if insufficient time is spent on making good the walls, giving them a base and then a top coat before ragging, stippling, dragging or stencilling. Women decorators should stick to a maximum 4 inch (10cm) brush for the base cover, or once laden with paint it will become too heavy to work quickly for long.

345 Most of the time white is the safest and best base colour for decorative finishes, and although rag-rolling can be very dramatic in stronger colours – in which case apply the darkest first – the patterns can appear to draw a room in, making it a lot smaller and darker than you intended.

346 Pale apricot, peach and bluish greys are currently fashionable and compatible with most furnishings. Professionals experiment with tubes of artists' paints, adding them to the top colour for greater variety and more subtle tones.

347 The choice of colour is yours, but the type of paint is important for the distinctive sheen in the finished product. Choose an oil-based eggshell for wood and a vinyl silk emulsion for walls, and get plenty of turps/white spirit for thinning it down.

348 The most important ingredient for special finishes is glaze, which acts as a fixative, stops the colour running and gives a more durable, slightly three-dimensional effect. Get it at specialist paint shops and builders' merchants, or order through DIY stores. You'll need equal quantities of paint and glaze.

349 To create clean, instant white borders, cheat by using any decorative painting technique over masking tape.

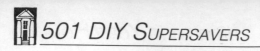

 Don't buy specialized badger brushes for decorative finishes – they cost a fortune. A wide, stiff bristle brush will give good results for dragging, and a rubber Artex pad for just a couple of pounds from DIY shops is just the thing for stippling.

See also 91–126.

○ *Ragging and rag-rolling . . .*

Ragging *is a technique where you bunch up a rag in one hand, press it into the paint and apply it to the walls, turning your hand in different directions to simulate a brocade pattern. For* rag-rolling *take a square of cloth, use two hands to hold it by diagonally opposite corners, and play about with it until it falls loosely into an untidy hammock shape. Dip it into the paint and roll it lightly over the wall, constantly changing direction. Always have a more than generous supply of rags, so you don't run out before the job is finished. It's the texture of the rag and the way it's rolled which give you the design. A single-size sheet torn up will cover an average-size room.*

351 Many decorators use the ragging technique and a sponge with satisfactory results, cleaning the sponge at frequent intervals with white spirit to keep the outline sharp. It must be a proper sea sponge and not the synthetic variety.

352 Use a combination of rag-rolling to cover the area quickly and ragging to add a variation in the pattern, or to introduce a two-tone effect where you fill in the gaps.

353 If two pairs of hands are available, the ideal is for one person to work ahead, applying a wide strip of colour, while the other follows, rag-rolling into the glaze. To avoid noticeable pattern changes space your breaks so that you don't stop until you reach a corner.

354 Remember that big patterns, using a loosely folded cloth, are best on larger areas, but for smaller designs – in bathrooms and bedrooms – tighten the fold. Don't grip the cloth, but let it roll freely, and when it becomes paint-logged and messy to work with change to a new one.

355 Glaze is a highly flammable material and the rags which come in contact with it should always be put in sealed containers before placing them in the dustbin.

356 The correct thickness of paint/glaze mix is important. Pour equal quantities into a paint kettle, blending really well with a paintbrush. Then add turps/white spirit a splash at a time until you have the consistency of thin cream.

 Dragging . . .

Here you deliberately emphasize brushmarks on wet glaze, using a dryish brush and removing some of the paint in the process. In small areas, using vertical strokes, dragging can give the impression of height. Along the tops and bottoms of doors, cornices and skirting, horizontal lines are preferable.

357 You can get an effect which is similar to dragging by using a comb with firm, well-spread teeth.

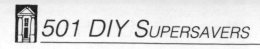

○ **Stippling . . .**

Use stippling to give a lacquered effect, like that on a speckled egg, on small areas, door panels, furniture and even lamp bases. The brush or rubber pad should be run over a dry cloth at intervals to prevent a build-up of paint which would blur the design.

 For larger areas – walls and floors – an old broom head with hard bristles is an extremely passable and quick method of stippling.

Restoring Old Beams

 Beams are often coated with bitumen – a shiny black stain. Use a hot air stripper to remove most of it, and work on the traces with a solvent paint remover and steel wool. You can then clean them up using petrol and with considerable caution (*see 386*). Many proprietary solvents are also petroleum-based but many times the price.

Bright Ideas

360 Many people are put off houses with a window which is over-looked by neighbours or has an unattractive view. Installing a stained glass window can solve the problem, and add to the charm (and value) of your home when you come to resell. *See also 186.*

Bad Guys: Draughts, Pests and Other Nasties

Draughts

 Stage a draught hunt on a windy day with a wet finger or a lighted candle, which will flicker near the point in windows, walls, floors or doors where the gale is coming in.

 Fit a brush-pile 'teeth' device over the inside of a letterbox opening, or buy a weighted or spring-loaded flap.

Fit a brush-pile 'teeth' device over the inside of a letterbox opening, or buy a weighted or spring-loaded flap.

If underdoor draughts are the problem, you can buy bristle strips, felt strip underseals and two-part devices for threshold and door bottoms to keep out wind and rain.

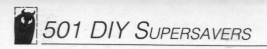

 To refix a self-adhesive draught excluder strip which no longer adheres, apply a thin coat of all-purpose adhesive to the surface on which you want to attach the excluder. When the glue is very nearly dry, press on the strip.

 Make a wind-stopping snake for a door bottom from a stocking filled with old tights, rags or scraps of polyester foam and decorate with material remnants, old buttons, bows etc.

 Block draughts around window frames (caused by shrinking timber) by filling the gaps with a non-setting mastic compound.

 Cover a working keyhole by fitting a brass escutcheon plate, or block an unused one with plasticine and cut out a cardboard cover to pin over it, which you can then decorate as you like.

 Altering the structure of your home to include draught lobbies inside front or back doors, or building a porch outside, will not only trap expensive heat but most likely add to the value of your property.

See also 80, 81, 128, 148, 321–22.

Condensation

○ *Prevention . . .*

 Stop excess moisture in the atmosphere at source. Oil and paraffin heaters give off one pint of moisture for every pint of fuel burned. Clothes drying and even human bodies add to the problem. Using automatic kettles and cooker hoods and putting lids on pans when cooking will all reduce steam. If your tumble dryer is not of the plumbed in, condensing kind, direct its exhaust outside by means of a flexible hose.

○ *Ventilation . . .*

370   Lack of ventilation – over-zealous blocking of fireplaces, sealing in heat round walls and doors, for example – makes condensation worse. If homes are well insulated to preserve heat, installing an extractor fan, or in severe cases a dehumidifier, should solve the problem.

371   Extractor fans must be positioned fairly high in a wall or window at the opposite side of the room to where air enters from the rest of the house. It needs enough power to give ten to twenty changes of air per hour for kitchens, and five to ten in bathrooms.

For damp around fireplaces see 483.

○ *Identification . . .*

372   Where damp appears on walls, you can find out where it's coming from in general by fixing a sheet of kitchen foil flush to the wall. If condensation is the problem, after a while water will collect on the surface of the foil rather than behind it.

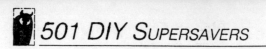

○ *Decorating . . .*

 Always allow newly erected walls or surfaces which have been recently replastered to dry out completely before decorating. In the case of a new house, allow six months.

 Ceramic tiles and gloss paint make a condensation problem worse. Choose a 'warm' surface of thermal board, expanded polystyrene, sheet cork or cork tiles.

 Adjacent strips of polystyrene (from wallpaper shops) should be overlapped slightly when hung. Cut with a sharp knife down a marked vertical line through the overlapped sheets, and peel off the excess. Use only emulsion paint or wallpaper to decorate.

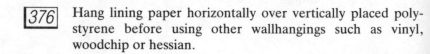 Hang lining paper horizontally over vertically placed polystyrene before using other wallhangings such as vinyl, woodchip or hessian.

○ *Floors . . .*

 Bed a small piece of glass in putty or plasticine, so that the glass is no more than ¼ inch (6mm) from the floor. If after twenty-four hours there is moisture on the underside of the glass, the problem is rising damp.

 Combat condensation on cold concrete floors by fitting nonslip cork tiles, wooden parquet blocks or a carpet with a foam underlay.

○ *Windows . . .*

379 Double glazing should effectively stop condensation on windows (*see 321–322*). As an alternative, drill some downward-sloping holes in the bottom frame. This allows drips to drain away and lets air in. You must, however, prepare the holes with wood preservative first to protect the timber.

380 If condensation forms between the panes in double glazing, remove the secondary glazing – whether on hinges or a sliding mechanism – and gently dry out every vestige of moisture with a hairdryer.

381 If the worst you have to cope with is the odd steamed up window, polish the pane with a little glycerine on a soft cloth.

○ *Bright ideas . . .*

382 In spare rooms, keep the doors shut to prevent cold and damp penetrating from other areas. Put a spare blanket on the bed. After two or three weeks the bed will still be dry, but the blanket – which will have drawn moisture from the atmosphere – will need airing.

383 Anti-condensation crystals are money down the drain. Tubs of salt and charcoal do a cheaper job of absorbing moisture in trouble spots. Dry out a damp cellar by dividing 2 lb (900g) of kitchen salt into four portions and placing each in a tin in one of the corners. The salt will draw out the moisture. When saturated, the tins can be dried out by standing them on a warm stove, making the salt usable for the same job again.

Rub a little bath oil over mirrors in bathrooms to prevent them steaming up.

385 Run cold water before hot in basins and baths. This reduces the risk of accidents and is kinder to acrylic bath surfaces.

Dry Rot and Fungus

386 Dry rot can be treated by painting it with petrol until it blackens and dies. As petrol is highly flammable, take care you don't do the same. Work in a well-ventilated atmosphere, and don't smoke.

 Treat mould or fungus on walls, stone floors, window frames etc. by wiping it away with neat household bleach before drying the area completely and treating it with a fungicide to kill the spores.

See also 308.

Pest Control

 Specialist companies dealing with rot and insect attack will give you a free survey. They will then quote for doing the job for you – advisable if it's extensive – or will supply the appropriate DIY products. Look under Pest and Vermin Control in Yellow Pages.

 Always wash any new piece of furniture which comes into your home in a strong ammonia and water solution.

390 Woodworm in beams and other structural timber: to find out if wood is infested, bore a hole using a power drill and a fine bit. If woodworm is active, very little pressure will be needed to cause brown powder to cascade out of the hole. Treat in early summer before the breeding season, with good liquid insecticide and an injector spray (available from DIY shops).

391 Woodworm in furniture can be coated with paraffin applied with a brush and allowed to soak in deeply. Use a knitting needle to poke it into bigger holes and treat for ten days, after which time the empty cavities can be filled with beeswax or melted paraffin wax.

392 Moths are allergic to lavender, cloves, oranges and cedarwood furniture. Kill off moth eggs in a carpet by using a hot iron over a damp cloth, and pressing until bone dry. *See also 492.*

393 To deal with flies, use vinegar as a rinsing agent when cleaning windows. Leave lemon and orange peel in their favourite haunts. Make a DIY fly strip by soaking lengths of brown parcel paper in equal parts of sugar and water, brought to the boil and cooled. Fumigate metal dustbins by burning newspapers or straw inside them.

394 The cheapest mosquito-repellent which also acts as a bite soother is citronella (from chemists). Alternatively burn citrus-scented candles in the house or garden. They are attracted by stagnant water, so make sure garden pools or rainwater tubs are not the problem.

395 Flies and mosquitoes hate mint, so rub a fresh sprig over your exposed parts when working out of doors.

396   Ants never cross a chalk line and aren't too keen on mint, cloves or turpentine. Lure them to a fatal trap of borax and sugar mixed. But, if small children and pets might get at it, pouring boiling water on nests is a safer, although only temporary, solution.

397   Mice are allergic to mint. Pop a few drops of essence of peppermint on cotton wool near mouse holes. For a trap bait, they prefer chocolate or peanut butter to cheese. Put traps (placed at right-angles to the wall) on newspapers to make it easier to bundle them up and dispose of them.

398   A simple but ingenious wasp bait needs a screw-top jar containing sugar, jam or honey dissolved in a little warm water. Pierce a few holes in the top with a pointed beer can opener, leaving gaps big enough for wasps to crawl in, but making it impossible for them to escape. Placing mothballs in an open trap away from their nest is likely to draw them out.

○   *Pets* . . .

399   For a DIY flea shampoo for dogs, mix one part Dettol or TCP with two parts washing up liquid and three parts water. Shake well before using. This mixture will store indefinitely.

If you add brewer's yeast to the animals' food the pores of their skin will give off an odour which repels fleas. Rubbing the fur with eucalyptus oil or vinegar on a damp chamois in between bathing sessions also works.

Plumbing and Central Heating

Preventing Problems

 Examine your waterworks. Just in case you need to call a plumber in an emergency, have his telephone number handy and when he arrives be able to point out where the supply is connected. Save his time and your money.

402 Open and shut stopcocks twice a year and lubricate them with oil or Vaseline to prevent them becoming jammed or corroded, so that even a small child's fingers could turn one in an emergency. Penetrating oil left on for fifteen minutes should loosen a stopcock which won't budge. Never leave it open to its fullest extent – even a quarter turn towards the closed position will prevent jamming.

403 Bleed the central heating pump of air when it has been out of use for any length of time. Run it for a couple of minutes each week throughout the summer to keep it in good working order.

404 Invest in a heat and light bulb, which costs very little to run but provides sufficient heat in cold lavatories and other unheated areas to prevent freezing.

405 Dripping taps should be repaired at all times to avoid water waste, but in winter especially. It will avoid water building up in the traps and waste pipes. A washer costs just a few pence.

406 Keeping a plug in the bath or sink in cold weather won't help when there is already water lying in the pipes. In extreme cold, add salt or anti-freeze to traps at night.

407 A few drops of glycerine in the lavatory cistern will act as an anti-freeze.

408　When going off on a winter holiday, it's best to drain the system completely, turning off the water supply and running the taps to empty the system. When you return, refill by opening the stopcocks and allowing the water to run freely for a minute to ensure against airlocks, before closing the taps.

First Aid
for Waterworks

409　Water expands by 10% when frozen and may split pipes, so locating the blockage as soon as possible and applying gentle thawing methods makes sense. Try a hairdryer or a hot water bottle. Alternatively, heat fire bricks in the oven and place as near the pipes as possible. If the pipe is outside, bind it with rags and pour boiling water over it.

410　An ever so slight drip from a cracked water pipe can be held in check for a while by rubbing soap in the crack to seal it and binding it with a paint-soaked rag. In the absence of paint, try Vaseline.

411　If the ball inside a cistern has cracked and filled with water, open the hole to let the water out. After rescrewing the damaged float cover it with a plastic bag, securely tied to seal it. It can now function again until a replacement is fitted.

412　If you have a central heating breakdown, run through the following checklist. Is the pilot light still on? Relight if necessary, following the manufacturer's instructions. Check the fuse on the main switch, possibly adjacent to the programmer, and check that the time switch is in the 1–2, 3–4 sequence. Check the boiler and room thermostats – it may not be cold enough for the system to have switched on. Are there air locks in the pump or pipes?

Fig Ⓐ
THE NUT

Fig Ⓑ
THE
SLEDGEHAMMER

Dealing with Difficulties

413   The best way to clean a drain cover is by burning off the debris. Throw it on a bonfire, and as an additional barrier against leaves etc. put a piece of chicken wire over the hole when the cover is replaced.

414   If you lose a small but precious object down the sink, don't panic. Get a bucket, place it under the U-bend of the outlet pipe under the sink, and arm yourself with a wrench. Release the nuts and empty whatever is trapped there into the bucket.

415   When water is coming out of a tap in fits and starts, or an air lock has stopped it completely, the best implement is a garden hose. Connect one end to the offending tap and the other to the mains cold tap (probably the kitchen cold tap). This should force air out when the kitchen tap is turned on. Turn it off when gurgling noises indicate that the water is starting to run. Disconnect the pipe and allow the water to run freely for a couple of minutes before closing the taps.

416 To unblock a sink, pour down a cup of neat washing up liquid and leave to soak for ten minutes. Next pour down generous amounts of hot water to clear the debris. Alternatively mix equal quantities of soda crystals and coarse salt and push this down, followed by boiling water and a cup of vinegar.

417 To unblock a loo, try an uncurled metal coat hanger to pull out the blockage. If that doesn't work, push a length of rubber hose down until it meets the blockage. Push and flush at the same time.

418 If you haven't got a proper plunger, improvise – use a mop with a plastic bag securely tied round its head.

419 When unscrewing taps to replace washers, put a cloth between the jaws of the spanner or pipe wrench to avoid scratching or damaging the surface and to give a better grip.

420 To unclog a showerhead, undo it and poke through the holes with a pipe cleaner. Soak the perforated part in neat vinegar overnight.

421 A DIY stopcock key can be assembled in an emergency from a long piece of stout wood (minimum 3 feet [90cm]) with a V-shape notched out of one end to a depth of about 3 in. Fix another piece of wood securely at the other end to make a T-shape handle. Now the stopcock can be opened by fitting the V-notch over it.

Save money on plumbers' bills and expensive caustic powders. Invest in a set of drain rods from a builders' merchant or DIY superstore. They will give years of service unblocking loos, gutters and downpipes.

Keep your emergency household candles in the fridge in winter. In the event of a power cut they will burn more slowly.

See also 472–477.

Electrics

Check Before
You Panic

 Before calling a service engineer, always check the plug, fuses and socket of any appliance.

 On washing machines and dishwashers that won't work, check the programme dials, then make sure that the outlet hose at the back isn't kinked, the outlet itself isn't blocked, and the filters aren't choked with food or fluff. One very common cause of an apparent breakdown is that the water supply has been turned off!

426 Checklist for a faulty vacuum cleaner. Is the bag too full or burst? Replace if necessary. Is the fanbelt caught up on something? Loosen and untangle it, or, if worn, buy another (from a hardware or electrical shop). It only needs two minutes and a strong wrist. Is the suction tube blocked or damaged? Push an uncurled coat hanger inside the tube to free anything trapped there.

427 Checklist for failed Christmas tree lights. Turn off the electricity, then make sure all the bulbs are screwed firmly into their sockets. Try a replacement bulb in each socket, switching on and off in between until they all light up. On British Standard sets, a partly white coloured lamp has a safety fuse and should only be replaced by another of the same kind.

Safety Measures

428 Never attempt any electrical job, however small, if you are overtired, unable to concentrate, or there are small children or pets around. Switch off and unplug any appliance before working on it.

429 Plastic, rubber, dry paper, wool and wood won't conduct electricity. Wear rubber boots when using electric lawnmowers, and rubber gloves when holding someone who has been electrocuted. If someone receives an electric shock, the first thing to do is turn off the current.

Basics

430 Keep in a handy place a selection of spare fuses, fuse wire, a small screwdriver, a good supply of candles, a torch with batteries which work and a spare torch bulb.

 Fitting a plug; green or yellow goes to earth, brown to live, blue to neutral. To help you remember on 13 amp plugs: bRown with an R in it goes to Right, bLue with an L in it goes to Left, and the earth wire always goes centre.

 If the light from a torch is dull, rub the positive terminal (the button part) with glass paper to aid the contact. But this is only a temporary solution – change the battery as soon as possible.

Bright Ideas

 Brasso is good for cleaning up dirty electrical switch plates or plug casing, where it would be dangerous to use water.

See also 444–483 for tips on saving electricity.

Recycling and Conserving Energy

New Ways
With Old Junk

434   Old floorboards can be cut up and made into window boxes. Use a few brass screws to secure the edges and drill drainage holes into the base. Give the exterior surface a coat of wood preservative, varnish or paint.

435   Assemble an instant bookcase in minutes from planks and concrete screen walling blocks. Use at least four planks – one on the very bottom to protect the floor from the rough bricks. The wood can be painted to complement the decor.

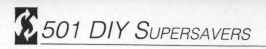
436 Make a garden table from an old door, stripped, weatherproofed with yacht varnish and placed on top of concrete screen walling blocks, cemented together.

437 Make headboards for beds from painted garden trellis, quilted material attached to a frame of copper piping, large mirrors or bookshelves. Hanging a rectangular bolster from a wooden curtain pole and rings is also most effective where the bed head is against a wall.

438 A great DIY barbecue requires fifty-eight bricks built in a hexagon design, an unwanted metal doormat and a grill from an old cooker.

439 Old-fashioned earthenware sinks, mounted on bricks, make brilliant containers for flowering plants and herbs.

440 The cabinet of a defunct grandfather clock can be fitted with shelves, to make a useful and good-looking cupboard for bathroom or bedroom.

441 An old trunk rescued from the attic becomes an attractive and useful piece of furniture when decorated. Try a coat of spray paint, or a remnant of leather, hessian or brocade cut to size and glued to the panels. Paint the hinges and locks with old gold or pewter leaf metallic paint, and add plywood partitions for storing records, bottles etc.

442 Build a dressing table in two minutes using two identical sets of drawers a chair's width apart, with a top (chipboard, laminate etc.) running across.

443 An old bicycle basket attached to the back of a cupboard door near the kitchen sink makes a terrific rubbish bag holder.

Saving Electricity

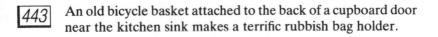

444 Fluorescent tubes may be more expensive to buy than 100 watt bulbs, but they last ten times longer and cost only half as much to run.

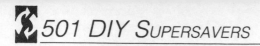

445 Install dimmer switches in conjunction with standard bulbs to prolong their life and cut the cost of the electricity needed to run them by as much as 75%. It's unlikely that you would have to alter your existing wiring.

446 Kettles and even kettle jugs always seem to produce more boiling water than required. Pour the extra into a thermos flask.

447 Instead of using a pre-soak and hot wash for dirty clothes, programme your washing machine for a shorter cycle at a lower temperature. Turn it off at the point where the water and soap are mixed through. Leave it to soak for a few hours or overnight for the dirt to dissolve. Switch back on to complete the wash. The clothes will be just as clean, but at half the cost.

448 By regularly defrosting your freezer – at least twice a year – you cut the cost of running it by 10%. To speed up the defrosting process next time, rub glycerine round all the inside surfaces before filling it again.

449 A freezer is at its most economical to run when full. To fill it up cheaply buy cut-price loaves at the end of the day at bakers and supermarkets. Fill milk cartons and margarine tubs with water to freeze for blocks of ice for cold boxes and to keep bottles cold in summer.

450 A shower saves hot water and so reduces your fuel bills – four or five people can shower in the same amount of water needed for a single bath.

451 Place a length of kitchen foil under your ironing board cover, shiny side up, and you'll get through the ironing in half the time. Using a brick rather than a metal stand as an iron rest further prevents heat loss.

 452 Electric fires with dirty reflectors waste heat. Use a silver polish on them for maximum brightness and cost-effectiveness.

Cutting Down Your Heating Bills

453 Help to maintain the efficiency of your central heating system with a professional service at least once a year.

454 Check that you're not overheating rooms and water. Each 1°C (about 2°F) change in the room thermostat setting, will make a difference of between 6 and 10% in your heating costs. Most people could lower it by a few degrees, wear extra clothing and still remain comfortable while saving money.

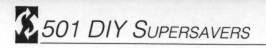

 Heating thermostats in a draughty hallway cannot work efficiently. A rush of cold air will produce a noticeable drop in temperature. They also react to heat spots, so don't install them near a record player, lamp or TV.

 If you fit individual thermostatic radiator valves to every radiator in your home, you can dispense with all other thermostats except the one on the boiler. Fit them when your central heating is installed, or at the annual service when the radiators are drained. They save heat by allowing each room to be controlled separately. Using 'free' heat from TV sets, cookers – even body heat from a group of people – can reduce fuel bills by a fifth.

 Electric storage heaters store heat at night at off-peak electricity rates. The heat is released into the room the following day and evening.

458 If you're away for long periods, consider fitting a frost thermostat to the outside of the house. This activates the heating system when the temperature drops to a very low level and the pipes are in danger of freezing.

459 Set your programmer carefully, to heat water and radiators before you get up in the morning and before you come home at the end of the day.

460 You don't need a high room temperature once you're in bed. Turning in thirty minutes earlier throughout the winter can result in a substantial improvement in heating costs and very likely in your health too. Keeping the heat on all night adds at least 15% to your heating bill.

 Use only radiator enamel to paint radiators – ordinary metallic paint reduces the heat flow.

462   Using radiator foil saves up to 15% of your heating bills. Taping kitchen foil to walls behind radiators and to the underside of shelves hung a few inches above them will reflect maximum heat back into the room.

463   Don't let curtains, carpets or furniture restrict the heat flow. *Long* curtains pulled over radiators merely heat the windowpanes (*but see 482*).

464   Blinds are often better than curtains at preventing heat loss, especially where a radiator is situated under a windowsill.

465   Oil for central heating tends to fluctuate in price. Apart from the possibility of a crisis in the world market, it falls in summer due to a decrease in demand. Check the cost at three local suppliers before placing your order. Discounts may be available on large quantities.

466   To make coal go further, dissolve a good handful of washing soda in a bucket of warm water and throw it over a hundredweight of coal when delivered.

○   *Loft insulation . . .*

467   Because hot air rises, you can save up to 15% of heat loss by merely unrolling 2 inches (5cm) of fibreglass insulating blanket in your loft, or packing with up to 4 inches (10cm) of the loose fill variety. In terms of saving fuel, the material will pay for itself in two years.

468   A house with a sloping roof and an attic needs insulating material fitted to the underside of the roof slope. Secure it with wire, or plastic trellis from a garden centre.

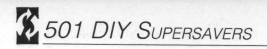

 Buy building paper to lay under blanket or loose fill insulating material. This will get into nooks and crannies where the blanket type is more difficult to fit, and will stop loose fill escaping.

 Fit an excluder round the edges of the loft hatch, and fix a piece of fibreglass roll on top of the trap door.

471 In long cold spells and especially when you leave the house, open the loft hatch for a while to let some warmth from below spread to the roof area.

O *Tanks and pipes . . .*

472 When the sales are on buy a jacket – or even two – for your hot water tank, and tape or tie it on well. You'll soon recover the jacket's cost by keeping hot water at the required temperature. Even a double layer of corrugated cardboard does the job if funds are low.

473 Insulate all pipes leading from the hot water cylinder to taps – a very cost-effective exercise, but often neglected.

474 Check that any hot water pipes below floorboards are adequately lagged.

475 Make a fitted jacket for the cold tank from off-cuts of insulating blanket, or buy pre-cut packs of 1 inch (2.5cm) sheet insulation. Secure with wire, string or tape. Remember to leave a gap underneath the tank to allow heat to rise to it from below.

476 Buy bandage-type insulator for pipes and secure with ties or tapes at intervals, or use the split-tube kind which you simply clip on, or tape at joints or bends. The latter is excellent for pipes which are hard to get to: all you do is shunt it into place.

477 Store off-cuts of fibreglass roll in a dustbin liner for patching up or filling odd corners later.

○ *Ceilings and walls . . .*

478 Polystyrene thermal foam ceiling tiles cover up cracks, stop heat escaping upwards and, as a bonus, reduce condensation and cut down noise from above. Fireproof ceiling tiles are available at little extra cost.

479 Sheets of polystyrene on walls and ceilings will not only keep heat in, but when coated with anti-condensation paint under emulsion or wallpaper will cut down moisture problems too.

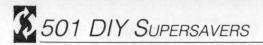

○ *Other heat loss . . .*

 For badly fitting windows, use a silicone-based sealant which comes in a plastic bottle with a nozzle. Squeeze a layer around the inner frame, close the window to press well in and then open it again until the sealant dries.

 Sheet polythene doubles as a safety measure and elementary double glazing. Clingfilm is a lot cheaper than proprietary window insulation packs which keep heat in and draughts out, and can be applied in minutes using only scissors and a hairdryer.

482 Snug-fitting, closely woven, *short* curtains, drawn at night, help keep in the heat (*but see 463*). Detachable linings convert summer drapes to winter weight.

483 Block off little- or never-used fireplaces. Fit and paint a plasterboard or plywood panel. Build in a ventilator to prevent damp, or have the chimney capped.

Save Money

484

Listening to a radio which is run on batteries is an expensive luxury. Even tuning in for only two hours a day would be forty times more expensive than using mains electricity. So here's one occasion where you can safely say: plug in and *save* money!

DIY Removals

485 The secret of a successful removal is to be organized. Start by planning weeks in advance and get between three and six quotes for the cost of hiring a van, to include packing cases and extras (e.g. hand trolley for bulky items). Establish the size of the van, the availability and cost. You can hire a driver by the day (twenty-four hours).

486 Make a list of people to inform of your new address. Include offices for car registration and driving licence. Depending on exactly where you are moving from and to, it may be necessary to contact the police and local highway authorities to arrange parking permission on the day.

487 Save well in advance bundles of newspapers and corrugated cardboard, cardboard eggboxes, sheets of polystyrene and packing boxes, plus plastic bags and dustbin liners.

488   Make sure you have more than adequate insurance cover. DIY removers tend to break more, and for this and other reasons you will not have the same indemnity as a company. Read the small print.

489   Your houseplants can travel in dustbins.

490   Put wet newspaper around everyday china and glass for better protection. It tightens as it dries, forming a protective case. Be careful, however, with good glass, as printers' ink could stain it. The acid in newspaper can also damage gilding on china. So use white tissue for your best stuff.

491   Pack larger garments round rolled up plastic bags – they will be less crumpled at the other end. Fill drawers with smaller items of clothing, bedlinen, towels and soft furnishings, and wedge small ornaments, pictures and other valuables safely in between the layers.

492   If soft furnishings or clothes are to be put in storage for some time protect them against moths by first airing and brushing them well, then wrapping them in layers of newspaper and storing tightly in boxes sealed with gummed paper.

Work out a colour code so that boxes and pieces of furniture can be marked to correspond with the colour labels you quickly attach on each door when you arrive at the new place.

 Keep maps, keys, an all-purpose cleaner and a cloth, kettle, cups, tea, coffee etc., washbag, tin opener, corkscrew, towel, loo roll, torch, first aid kit and any other indispensables in an emergency box.

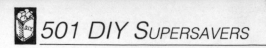 Put aside, in individually labelled dustbin liners, each child's night things, duvet and favourite toys. Pack these items last, so that they are the first to be unloaded at your destination.